AF445511

Dedicated to my Dad,
Who said "I'm proud of you, son."
And my Mom,
Who always supported me.
"Honour thy father and thy mother"
(KJV Exodus 20:12)

Contents

Forward

I first met Anthony when he was 11 and invited me for an interview. He had a home school project he was working on that would help him to learn more about the community that is Palmer AK. He was able to interview a fair number of city leaders in order to learn the heart of Palmer. Fast forward to today, he is halfway to a college degree desiring to be a creative writer. This book is proof of his creativeness. Through glimpses of Palmer history using poetry, Anthony truly reveals his love for Palmer. As a 20-year resident of Palmer, I thank him for sharing that love with me as well as with you in a way that only he can do.

Frank Emrick
Teacher of Alaska Studies
Alaska Bible College

Proem for Poems

Read of the painter,
Read of the farmer,
Read poems about,
Fair little Palmer,
We are prosaic,
But some of the time,
We are romantic,
Like houses of brick,
You a sourdough,
Or a cheechalker?
Enjoy my Palmer's,
Bright, storied, pyre,
Take every poem,
And give it your mind,
To consider, grind,
Out something to ply,
But don't think too hard,
I'm genius in part,

Not at all in whole,
I've no critics heart,
Can't say what'll be done,
Will my poems last,
Like the midnight sun,
Or like winter's one?
To whatever end,
Is around the bend,
Fame or fortune comes,
I'll write to His end.

Let's All Go To 203 Kombucha
"This place is amazing,
Thank you for creating,
Such a wonderful community"
"It's the place to be"
"Thanks for making me an addict"
"Thanks and congrats"

"Cheers to many years to come"
"Safe, intellectual, and fun"
"Best toast, best drinks, best vibes"
"Palmer wouldn't be the same without you,
neither would I"

"So happy to have you in our community,
For all the good vibes and energy"
"You make our town even better"
"So glad you are here in Palmer"

"The hot chocolate and vibes are amazing"
"This is a second home to our family"
"Cheers to all that lies ahead"
"You guys are the best!!!"

This poem is a *found poem* meaning it is made up of quotes that I found. The quotes and the way I used them pay homage to the establishment which hosted the event that started this book: 203 Kombucha. At 203 they have a poster full of encouragement and gratitude from their 3-year anniversary. I believe this was the third poem I ever presented at their open mic night, put together about five minutes before my turn came up to go on stage.

It is easy on the editing side of things, none of the quotes are changed from what you will find on the poster. But, while these may be other people's words, combined they make up my words to describe 203, and they have made the words of Palmer. It is not just an individual, but a community.

The Three Log Churches
German, Latin, and the Scott,
Vicarious, they all sought,
To worship as they were taught,

Government did not think,
That they'd all praise out of sync,
But harmonize for red ink,

One building was offered all,
For their Mass worship withal,
The Protestant altar call,

But the people acted out,
What they thought was most devout,
To avoid a worship's drought,

They built up churches, triune,
At their own cost, to their tune,
Cultivating praise to bloom,

Thus was grown community,
Where separate melds unity,
'mongst those who praise Trinity.

The Government, when Palmer was being developed, offered all the colonists supplies to build one church, which was not found to be acceptable. Catholics, Presbyterians, and Lutherans all have differences that affect how they conduct a Sunday service or mass. Due to these differences the Colonists ended up building two additional houses of worship for themselves. The only building to keep its original frame is the United Protestant Presbyterian Church, affectionately known as The Church of a Thousand Trees.

Since this poem is focused on churches, I wanted to make some appropriate references. I used gardening terms because those appear a lot in the Bible, vicarious starts with Vicar which is a term for the priest's role, and triune is close to Trinity, to name a couple things.

The Art Cafe
Oil stained the floor, grease coated the walls,
The sounds of industry once filled its halls,
A realm where but one was free to create,
A realm that car lovers appreciate,

But in 2018 it was renewed,
Some ladies came in and gave it to you,
The people who wish to paint on their break,
Fulfilling your nature, to rest and make,
We're made in His image, made to reflect,
The One who created life near perfect,

So come and drink some nice coffee or tea,
Take a bite of the fudge or the ice cream,
Paint a ceramic, tile mosaics,
And leave the mess, they're happy to clean it.

The Art Cafe was started in an old autobody workshop, but when I first visited, I found that instead of old cars it was full of clay figurines, posters from bygone state fairs, and beautiful antiques, including a yellow chair fastened high up on the wall. I almost wrote a poem about the chair, but there was only so much I found to write about, so I decided to ask more questions about the place till I found something that made sense to me to write about.

They are very friendly over there, eager to give you a tour of all the options for art that they offer. Their fudge is delicious, and their chai lattes are pretty good too, I can't speak on any of their other foods and drinks, but they certainly look and smell good.

Alaska Gifts

Walk through the door, find yourself at the bank,

Where carpet is moored and room ain't blank,

The little bear in his hat guides you forth,

"Follow the stones rare flow, where nature morphs,

Morphs from wilds tone to artists design,

Follow the whale's drove and the salmon's dive",

So, you follow the path and are welcomed,

By etched glass, and diamond willow,

Set aside for wine and set for candle,

In state designed, not lower state handled,

If your futures cold there's sweaters to buy,

In backroom holds where their creator lies,

The first leg is done, you've traveled quite far,

The next thirds quite fun with its honey jars,

And if you're bored, you'll find crafts on your right,

You'll make a seahorse, or eagle in flight,

There are many stories to tell on shelves,

Forget your worries and tell one yourself,

Now you've reached the end of silvertip store,

Just how you begun, on stone waters shore,

Take your pick of the Barnacle sauces,

The wick burns low on your free finances,

But with the waxes last drop buy a knife,

And don't be lax, get your friend something nice,

Your journeys not ended, it's halfway done,

You're not quite finished, there's still so much sun,

You still must return to who guided you,

Whose wisdom unspurned, 'stead, followed through,

Leave through the door but don't forget the bear,

Thank him once more, petting his wooden hair.

Alaska Gifts conveys a journey through a store that is either referred to as Alaska Gifts or Silvertip, depending on who you ask. They just didn't change the street sign when it became Alaska Gifts. All the items in this store are produced by Alaskan craftsmen, artists, and companies, so none of the products were "lower state handled." They are also one of the most generous stores to the local creator. Most stores will only pay the artist when the art is sold, but Alaska gifts pays the artist upfront.

Alaska Gifts has one of the most beautiful floors in Palmer, a stone mural that flows throughout the building, with salmon jumping and a pod of whales welcoming customers right at the start. They also have a wood carved bear at the front door greeting people, Hence a lot of the descriptions

Bright Lights Book Project
Free books,
Free books,
Free books,
Take your pick of what to read books,
You get to keep all and each books,
Enjoy the cute bunny kid books,
Or brighten your light with big books,

It helps the mind to grow and bloom,
When what's printed on spruce wood
loomed,
Is used to fuel the light upstairs,
Glowing bright as aroura's flares,

Don't fear contrary looking books,
Like Captain Beatty who cooks books,
But like Guy Montag, keep these books,
And take your pick of the free books,
Free books,
Free books,
Free books.

Throughout Palmer's various small businesses, there are shelves full of books with a little poster on the side. When I first discovered the poster, I was drawn like a moth towards a light, in big bold letters it read "Free books, Free books, Free books." Which sounded to me as free beer would to an alcoholic.

Books are as valuable as a large salmon run and feeds the mind just as well as the salmon feeds the belly. Though the quality of the salmon varies, and occasionally some are found rotten and putrid on the beach, the vast majority have many nutrients to offer. Only when the salmon is consumed do we receive the benefits that it offers, so you ought to read.

Bishops Attic II
Outside the Attic, trees sparkle,
Crystal coating made her smile,
As she placed into a small bag,
Baby clothes which made the mom glad,
Onesies, booties, and cute knit hats,
New to the mom, loved in the past,
She watched the mom leave with a sigh,
Whose husband worked morning to night,

Next in the line came an old man,
With naught but pure salt on his head,
His smile showed bars like a cage,
Exposing his tongue as a knave,
He placed before her a thick coat,
Seven bucks even, he 'bout broke,
Twas all he had, the warmth to hold,
He paid, then plunged into the cold,

Third in line, 'fore she recovered,
Was her sister and her brother,
They easily bought two antiques,
For the white elephant next week,
Something ugly she would avoid,
If she happened to have a choice,
They departed with warm "good day,"
Then she left the Bishop to pray.

Bishop's Attic is a thrift store in downtown Palmer that is affiliated with St. Michael's Parish. It is technically Bishop's Attic II, the first one is in Anchorage, Alaska, founded by Archbishop Joseph T. Ryan back in 1971. The proceeds from Bishops Attic go to support the Parish and other non-profits throughout the valley. In an article in the December 2023 edition of *The People's Paper* it was revealed that they have given $450,000 to the community.

I wanted to write a poem with a narrative for this one. Most of my poems were experiential, or had a loose narrative, but this one is much more structured, and gives a more complete story. Given that one reason for Bishop's Attic to exist is to assist those less fortunate I wanted to have a focus on those, but there are also plenty of people who are there for a good deal, hence the last pair of people.

Lazy Mountain

Up and up and up we go.
Down down down. . . down, our feet slip.
We are traveling three miles now,
Five miles distance by the end.

Peak of Lazy is our goal,
Its rocky cliffs and Old Glory,
We'll look on the world below,
So up and up we do go.

From a distance, seems relaxed,
But then we climb on its back,
Angle sharp, sixty degrees,
Up and up, the peak we'll see.

Down, down, down, the mud pushes,
Three thousand feet yet to rise,
On this poorly named mountain.
Up and up and up we climb.

Down, down, the mountain fights back,
Though we still reach timberline
A thousand more feet to climb,
Up and up and up we rise.

Down we all suddenly slip,
Mud then switches to solid rock,
The Alphorn declares the top,
So now we travel up, up.

At the end we cheer and roar
We stand above where hawks soar.
gaze upon Mat-Valley's floor
We're triumphant evermore.

Lazy is one of the more popular mountains to hike in the Valley. Its name may be derived from a story where the farmers burned down trees rather than chopping them down, to save effort and, in effect, be lazy, however, I have not yet been able to find records that support this claim. Whatever the reason for naming it Lazy Mountain, you are not being lazy if you choose to hike up it, the beginning of the hike is at an unusually steep incline, and is often made up of slick, saturated, surmountable mud.

At the top of the peak there are three items to take note of, one is made of PVC, one is made of fabric, and the last one is made of paper, the poem reveals what these are, so I needn't describe them here. You could also go and see these things and enjoy the amazing view by hiking up it yourself.

Matanuska Eternal

They named me Matanuska
It does not matter to me.
I'll do what I've always done,
Even long after their spirits go free.

I take the silt far down stream,
Far away from the glacier
Which is the cold source of me,
And hand it off to my sister, Knik

Once, they tried to slow me down,
Dumped brass and aluminum,
Into my swift peaceful flow
I would not be stopped and took those
coins far.

Perhaps one day I will stop,
Perhaps the glacier will end,
But none of you will be there,
I will last long past what your future's cast.

The Matanuska River divides the Butte from Palmer with the only crossing being George W. Palmer bridge. The river flowed when the first settlers arrived, when the colonists began coming, when I arrived, and it will continue to do so. There is no reason for me to believe that in my lifetime or the lifetime of my children it will cease to flow. The river is older than any of us and it will last longer than any of us. This feeling of continuance was a focus of mine, nature always outlasts us, our days will always be numbered less than the beauty we admire in Alaska.

There is a mention of dumping coins in the river, those are the Bingle coins, if you can gather a full set, I have heard they sell for thousands of dollars. Best of luck finding them, for they are all either in collector's hands or in the river's hidden stash.

Coal Black Train
Engine number five rests,
Living out retirement,
Under Palmer shelter,
Too True,

Older journeys done now,
Engine Five entertains,
Those she counted as her,
New crew,

Children clamber cheerful,
Each one careless, fearless,
Swinging in the window,
Yoohoo.

Engine Number Five has always been an attraction to the youth. I have seen them clamber all over it, climbing up some of the wheels and pistons to get onto the roof. I have seen them play pretend, and imagine themselves a train engineer, pulling at the many levers, ensuring the train gets to its imaginary destination on time. I was once one of those kids too, moving whatever lever could still be adjusted, allowing me to speed down the imaginary tracks.

The structure that I chose for this poem has a rhythm to it: "ENgine NUMber FIVE rests." This was to imitate the pounding of the pistons as the train moves. The final line in each stanza I made to sound like that classic train call of "choo choo." The result is a structure that imitates the noises children make when they pretend they are a train, which is the whole life of Engine Number Five now.

In Honor of the Soldier in the Stone
I saw your stone as I passed by,
Sad metal plaque of a proud guy,
The words inscribed give your late name,
Your last name was Woods, your first,
Shane,

When I was young and learning math,
You served your country in Iraq,
Where you stood and fought every day,
In honor we write K.I.A.,

Who were you beyond a soldier?
Were you a husband or a father?
Were you alone when you passed on?
Or are your brothers, with you, gone?

I am unaware, I don't know,
But I go and I see your stone,
Son of this Alaskan Valley,
We all salute your last sally.

It is always tragic when a loved one is lost in war, no matter what is felt about the war itself. There is not much revealed about Shane Woods from the memorial that rests near the train depot in Palmer, only that which is necessary for you to know that he was one of ours, and that he served, and that he died serving.

If I had done more research I would have been able to answer all the questions that were posed in my poem, but part of my poem is asking the unanswered questions that I initially had, and the feeling of being empty of knowledge.

In a way, the lack of knowledge that I had allows Shane W. Woods to not only be his own person but also to transcend into the essence of being a symbol. A symbol for those veterans who's lives were taken in service to our home. My heart goes out to the families of the Shane Woods in the world

Rainy Friday

I sat on the bench and listened to them
play,
Sweet melodies that matched all the rain,
The wind came through and tossed my hair,
A playful gust pulling through the wet air,
The clouds were gray and filled the sky,
Giving everyone a melancholy time,
A time that matched the band that played,
Blues were heard at the fling today.

The Friday Fling is a key part of Palmer in the summer. Starting in late spring and ending the week before the State Fair. Local musicians will let their art flow throughout the fling, affecting the mood (with the lady selling ocarinas interjecting with her own musical thoughts). Food trucks will line the street, with everything from burgers to Asian cuisine are offered. It is a miniature cacophony of smells as well as sounds, all offering what the locals have produced.

When I was writing this poem there was a blues band playing that day, and I quite forgot to write down their name. I don't even remember what song they were performing, I just remember that it was raining. I took that isolated memory and put it to verse.

Car Launch Countdown
Remember your liberty and community,
Don't forget what it means to be an,
American and Alaskan,
As you watch, north of Palmer,
Trucks and cars flying off,
Over the cliff face,
Hear freedom rev,
On your marks,
Get set,
Drive.

One of the strangest ways to celebrate Independence Day is found just north of Palmer: the Car Launch. It is exactly what it sounds like. If you want to see it in person, make sure to show up early, otherwise you will have to hike quite a way to the location.

When I was trying to figure out how to write a poem about this event, nothing fitted the vibe. But on one of my walks, as I threw various ideas at my mental dart board, one idea struck a bullseye: a single phrase "on your marks, get set, go." I began asking what where the qualities of this phrase, and one of them is that it was a countdown in two ways, intention, and syllable. From there I developed the idea of creating a countdown that starts with ten syllables and goes down to one: 10, 9, 8, 7. . . etc. It fits quite well, especially changing the end to "drive" which was better than the original change of "fly."

Winter has Come

Winter has come, Palmer's at rest,
A cold blanket lies on her breast,
The bears have gone into their dens,
Not till spring will they wake again,
All of nature has gone to sleep,
Only awake the chickadees,

Winter has come, Palmer's at rest,
Except for humans full of zest,
Seasonal work takes a long break,
Fishermen are now forced to wait,
So anxious they sit on the ice,
Hoping the hole'll offer some bites,

Winter has come, Palmer's at rest,
So come now, please do your best,
To understand what has been seen,
From nature you may partially glean,
There is value in your waiting,
Cease your minds constant berating,

Winter has come, Palmer's at rest,
Except for colorful Christmas,
I understand our Savior's born,
So, celebration can't be scorned,
But we fight His true intention,
"God rest ye merry gentlemen."

This poem has gone through the most iterations of any in this book. I could never seem to get it right, the only thing that stayed the same was the repeating idea "winter has come. . . at rest." It used to read "the worlds at rest" but even that had to go. There also used to be an entire extra stanza, but it didn't fit, and so had to go. I've been told that good writing is not what you add, but what you take away, but I do not recall where the original quote came from, only that a teacher of mine was fond of it.

There are varying kinds of rest that one can achieve, physical, mental, spiritual, and imaginary. That last one is often what people pursue, because it is a lot easier to escape into something shallow and imaginary, than to put in the effort to get true rest. I would encourage you, dear reader, to put in the effort to find how to truly rest.

The Library's Scar

Look at the scar that has pierced through
her head,
As the librarians look on in dread,
The cold snows pour in on her paper ward,
Too much damage has been done to just
board,
It up till springtime brings a chance to fix,
A chance to undo winter's weighty tricks.

A new warden was chosen to defend,
All the paper treasures of his old friend,
Though he's still quite young comparatively,
For 40 years stood the old Valkyrie,
But now he shall hold fast 'gainst the
weather,
He hopes the storms shall strike him like
feathers.

As for the old Valkyrie's wounded form,
She lies there wholly abandoned, forlorn,
They outlined her in ugly, yellow, tape,
Waiting to heal her on a later date,
But till then read her obituary,
Here doth lie Palmer Public Library.

Growing up, the Palmer Public Library was one of my favorite places to be. I would dive into the kids section and devour every bit of writing that I could, but in early 2023 something else dived into the kids section.

Alaska winters can be hard, and the amount of snow can become quite heavy. Most roofs are sharply slanted so that the snow will slip off before any damage is dealt to the building, but apparently the Palmer Library was not slanted enough. During closed hours, the Library's roof caved in right over where the kids books were kept, snow poured in, and the building was shut down, the library moved.

As of the writing of this the Library is temporarily in another building with plans to build a new structure in the near future. I did not make it to the planning meeting, so I am not currently privy to the selected design, and I doubt I will know anything till the rest of Palmer knows.

Valkyries Burial

They have finally begun to dig her grave,
After looting the treasure that we gave,
Into her charge, to protect and to save,
And I visited her to give due praise,

The air was cool, and the trees were
changing,
Like dried drops of blood, the leaves sat,
framing,
Her sorry form, a yellow claw tearing,
My childhood memories, despairing,

She was once a majestic Valkyrie,
Who raises me not to where warriors feed,
But to where Shakespeare, Twain, Spenser,
and Keats,
With Longfellow and Poe write, build, and
read,

Will she receive honor when her they've
thrown,
Into the trash, by monument or stone,
Or will they leave unmarked her concrete
bones,
So that her service will become unknown?

As I watched I felt a tear touch my eye,
And vanish in the rain, fallen from sky,
In time it was lost, soaked in ground it lies,
Much like the Valkyrie who before us, died.

On one of my walks I noticed that there was an excavator tearing down the section of the Palmer Public Library that had suffered the aforementioned scar. At this point I had already written the poem lamenting *the Library's Scar*, but I did not know what the plan was moving forward. Would they demo the building? Would they rebuild it? Was the temporary building going to be made permanent? I didn't know the answer to any of these questions, all I did know was that they were destroying the place that I loved.

I had called the Library a Valkyrie in my last poem, so I decided to run with that idea in this poem. I have also since found out that they are planning on rebuilding the library, which will be the subject of a future poem that will probably include Fenrir, since the company in charge of the project is named Wolf Architecture.

Palmer's Whistle
Can't you hear the whistle blowing,
Rise up so early in the morn,
8am the work starts a flowing,
Palmer is kind enough to warn,

At noon you hear the whistle sound,
For you to eat and spend money,
Like Yankee Doodle went to town,
A riding on his white pony,

At 5pm say "what the heck",
Let's all go home and not forget,
My job and little bitty check,
Six pack and television set.

As long as I can remember Palmer has had a whistle blown three times a day. It can be heard throughout the whole town and indicates the three aspects of the historical work day: start work, lunch break, end of the work day. The whistle appears to originate from the Palmer Fire Station, a deduction I made from going on walks nearby around the time of the second whistle.

Since the whole point of the whistle was to establish work hours for everybody back in the day, I decided to take bits of American folk or country songs that seemed to be related to that aspect of the work day. Half of each stanza is inspired by, or directly sourced from, one of those songs, the other half is completely from my own hand. Part of the reason for me to go the route of those songs was because historically a lot of music was made to entertain during the mundane work.

Wilughoyuk
Wilughoyuk, the sea shrew mouse,
A creature that on hunters will pounce,
A terror that burrows straight through,
What they wear on their foot, boot or shoe,
It skitters around on their skin,
And if they move it burrows in,
And plunges straight into their heart,
Cleaving body and soul apart,

When we see this man what to do?
One with worn coat and hole filled shoe,
Their minds are ever on the mouse,
They may hate it, but can't get out,
"Please, my nose has begun to itch,"
They plead as they begin to twitch,
They need something to keep them calm,
Something to make the threat seem small,

Some hear this and respond "your pain,
Comes from the mouse, clear out that
lane,"
Others offer to itch their nose,
But no other help they propose,
So, they leave him as a slave,
To the whims of a mouse, his grave,
But what can you expect from them,
Few have ended the mouses whim,

What of the young women who face,
The sea shrew mouse within this place?
If pretty, they're offered an out,
By akemkumiu who spout,
Liberation through surrender,
And by loved ones who demean her,
To brush off the mouse she faces,
And wear in place, shame and cages,

Troubled numbers will only grow,
As mice feed on the crumbs we sow,
Thousands will die frightened and bound,
If their freedom cannot be found,
But it's a struggle when the mouse,
Will eat them from the inside out,
It's no wonder that few escape,
And numbers only escalate,

For since I traveled to the south,
These sea mice infested my house,
Within Palmer's mountainous walls,
Many shiver along paved halls,
One or two when I left the door,
But on my return, so much more.

This poem does not offer any solutions, but it addresses a real problem. If I knew a solution that was not already being done then I would offer it here, but maybe that is something I will come across in the future. All I can say now is that it breaks my heart, and it feels like people are quite ignorant of certain aspects of the issue.

I wanted, in this poem, to say what is going on through references to mythology. Great poets will often reference Greek or Roman myth to artistically convey an idea to the reader. I think this has been done to death. What I decided to do was to search the internet for Alaskan mythological creatures and find one that best represented the problem in a metaphorical sense. I did this because I am an Alaskan, living in Alaska, writing about an Alaskan town, and I do not want to go halfway around the world to find something to tell us about ourselves.

Under Palmer Town
Deep down, under Palmer town,
What you think's bound to be found?
The dirt which makes up the ground?
true, but there's more that's around,

As Eagle flies through the sky,
Man swims where light doesn't shine,
Deep down under Palmer town,
A pool's beneath eagle's crown,

Your left, a BANG, your right? PING,
Drink your ale and hear it ring,
Deep down under Palmer town,
A gun range sits 'neath the House,

Bend your back to take the path,
The way Inn's been sealed at last,
Deep down under Palmer town,
Colony's tunnels' shut down,

When you look down at your feet,
Consider what may lie 'neath,
Deep down under Palmer town,
Derelict places abound.

Tunnels lie underneath Palmer's historical district, sealed up, hidden away. One day they may be opened again, allowing for people to reserve a spot on a tour to explore the underground places. The original intention for the tunnels was for water pipes, since, if they ever needed repair, it would be easier to go into the tunnels than having to dig up the frozen ground. It also allowed teachers staying at the Colony Inn to go to the school without having to step into cold winter. There are a couple of other notable things beneath our town, a pool and a gun range, both out of commission, but functional at one point.

I do not overtly tell you where some of these things are, but the clues are there in the poem, and not very well hidden at that. I have yet to see any of these myself, but this is what my research has turned up. Who knows what else may be hidden under Palmer that I am, as of yet, unaware of.

Borough Building
You once were a school establishing rules,
Rules of nature and rules of thought,
Winter grew cold, you gave warm soup to
hold,
The children were thankful a lot,

Now you've changed your path from English
and math,
You've given your books to others,
Now your over Palmer infrastructure,
And justice properly fettered,

To show your reign you're built with pearly
frame,
No other building quite like you,
Standing tall, head and shoulders above all,
Clearly king of buildings you view,

Whether within they're wise or hide 'neath guise,
And turn against what they ought be,
Whatever is viewed, reader, is up to you,
You vote for whoever may lead.

There were a lot of potential stanzas that I was working on for this poem, including one that would compare the Borough Building to the White House, but none seemed to work well. Some were too controversial for an author's first work, others were disjointed and mangled, like the victim of a bear attack. What you see before you is the final result of all that editing.

"And justice properly fettered" might seem odd, fettered means restrained or restricted, and that is what we need a justice system for. What we see when there is no formal justice system is people taking revenge, and that vengeance is often far to extreme for the circumstances. For an example, look at Lamech's declaration to his wives in Genesis 4:23-24, he had nothing that restrained him, and so he killed a man for a wound that was dealt to him. We need justice systems that do not go as far as we *feel* they ought to.

Open Mic Waltz
Faces all focused on,
People showcasing their,
Local creations here,
Playing their local flare,

Poetries spoken by,
Lloyd with his voice so fine,
Sharing experience,
Mostly events gone by,

Gregor and Mike at the,
Mic with their classic tunes,
Mike is percussion while,
Gregor's guitar strings move,

Many others have fun,
Showing what each has done,
'Cluding Scott Lewis who's
Dancing 'neath midnight sun,

join us by signing your,
Name on the dotted line,
Giving music or rhyme,
All will support this night.

This poem was requested by a local musician who frequently plays at the open-mic night at 203 Kombucha. Each of the people named are real, and, as of writing this, are still frequent performers every Friday.

There are several other artists who display their works. Many of the songs and poems that are performed are originals by them, though there are plenty of good covers as well, such as Gregor and Mike's classic tunes. Occasionally other skills besides music are offered, such as Lloyd's poetry, though we have yet to see much else up on stage.

It was hard finding the right structure to write in. What I settled on was a structure that imitates the musical form of a waltz. If you can, pay attention to where the syllables are naturally stressed, it should feel like the musical count **1** 2 3, **1** 2 3, etc.

Palmer's Metal Model
Palmer water tower,
Icon in the valley,
Quickly built in five days,
Three men rarely photo'd,

Train arrived on day one,
Then begun the fun task,
From Seattle given,
To the Palmer col'ney,

Swiftly came the fifth day,
Ninety plus seven foot,
Stood before the Mat'nu,
Waters flow down townward,

Nineteen sixty was when,
It retired serving,
Palmers water for the,
Chance for metal modeling.

All tourists capture,
Photos showing Palmer,
Written all across her,
Metal water tower.

When I went to the Palmer Visitor Center and Art Museum to ask them for ideas of what to write my poems about, this is one of the things they mentioned. They gave me a few facts for me to play with, and I went off to do a little additional research.

One of the bits of history I was told was how fast the tower was built. When writing this poem, I wanted to reflect that speed and so I chose to reduce my usual number of syllables from 8-10 to 6. Another consideration that went into play with this poem is that a friend of mine mentioned before that he preferred poems that had no rhyme to them, so with his words echoing in my mind I produced this.

There is a New Day, And This is It!
"There is a new day, and this is it!"
said colonists as they sat transfixed,
upon the shores of Alyeska,
ready to farm the Matanuska.

"There is a new day, and this is it!"
Shouted all the homeless in their tents,
As their first house was being built up,
Just as winter's frost was at its cusp.

"There is a new day, and this is it!"
Came the farming family's cry, with bliss,
As their first buds burst out of the ground,
Breaking through the Great Depression's
mound,

"There is a new day, and this is it!"
 Cackled the government as they mixed,
Up the currency with which they paid,
Where once was the dollar, Bingles laid.

"There is a new day, and this is it!"
Cheered the barman as he gladly lift-
-ed a sign accepting Bingle coin,
And with his loud cheer the people joined.

"There is a new day, and this is it!"
Muttered stone mason as he carved this,
Phrase into rock so that all would know,
The hope with which Palmer did grow.

I was taking one of my routine walks around Palmer when I found myself amongst several engraved stones. Three of the stones had the names of all 203 families which made up the initial colonists, but one of the stones had a single phrase carved into it "there is a new day and this is it, the Matanuska Colony" there was no author to attribute the quote to, and a quick Google search brings up nothing as to a potential source. The stones had been there as long as I can remember, and I can remember a long time.

I wanted to make sure the phrase was used in several different contexts to give it a bit of variety. I went through some of bits of history that Palmer experienced that felt like they would fit with the words, some of the stanzas got cut, but most of them stayed. I wrote the last one, desiring to give my reader a bit of encouragement.

Two O' Three Founders

Depression seized the country,
Many stuck in poverty,
Including those 2 0 3,
From three states and their counties,

Though the ground they never tilled,
They still drove tractors up hills,
All so that they could pay bills,
Till they're offered "The New Deal",

2 0 3 families signed,
And as they waited in line,
They thought how to tell a lie,
That they truly qualified,

"Ya'll are farmers, yay or nay?"
Government men said that day,
2 0 3 chose then to say,
"Yes, we all know fruit and grain",

Even though they told a fib,
Very quickly they were shipped,
To Palmer, a land that dipped,
Between mountains snowy tip,

There they met with bitter news,
Government words meant to sooth,
Promised "homes with mountain views",
But forest land was the truth,

So, if you're offered a hand,
Don't lie to get a few grand,
But keep in mind "New Deal's" plan,
Give bad farmers wooded land.

I was told, during a tour of Palmer's historical district, that a large number of the families who signed up for the Matanuska Colony barely had any farming experience. There were a few who succeeded, some due to quick learning, others from previous experiences to draw on, but the majority could only produce low quality vegetables. This led to the Bingle, and to some replacement colonists coming up (though there is more nuance to it).

When the Colonists came, they had been promised a lot more than they got. Almost none of the land was cleared, none of the houses were built, and almost none of the timber they cut down was usable. The majority of them had to stay in tents because there was no other choice, and a tent in winter is a difficult experience.

The First Good Egg
In Palmer's early bubble,
A Polish couple,
Purchased chickens for to raise,
Food to aid their days,

Chickens are small and lightweight,
A nice easy freight,
And produce both eggs and legs,
To feed in many ways,

But the eggs were perilous,
Heard Vickaryous,
The Polish ones with the eggs,
Which were freshly laid,

So, they sought to find what made,
The problem 'fore laid,
Why did their eggs taste funny,
But shipped ones yummy,

So, they cracked one right open,
Punched by aroma,
Sulfurous were those shipped here,
But theirs left good air,

Palmer was soon made aware,
Bad they had all year,
Their health paying the toll,
Good tasted awful.

One of the things we often take for granted in our lives is how quick shipping is, and how refrigeration has helped us in preserving our food. Back in the colony days whenever eggs were shipped up to Palmer, they would go bad before being sold. What is more surprising is that nobody realized that the sulfuric smell was not a bad sign. When the Vickaryous' started selling freshly laid eggs the people thought that those eggs had gone bad because they were used to rotten ones.

There is a certain truth I thought of with this story: if people have nothing but bad that surrounds them, it is easy to think that good is instead awful. Usually though, after a proper taste of what the good has to offer, people are naturally drawn to return to it, but sometimes that's not how things play out.

A Taste
You ever studied Palmer history?
It's a test with many controversies,
The government sent two O three families,
To farm, to feed, mining communities,

At our first school segregation was cut,
Which put the heads of D.C. in a rut,
However, to make up for this good touch,
They treated logistics like a cruel crutch,

In a show of historic off-rhyme,
The Govs once fought business with Bingle coin,
Then in twenty-one it came back in time,
To fight collapse from Covid one nine,

There is just a taste of what Palmer's done,
The heritage of its daughters and sons,
What comes next is the guess of anyone,
The future is His 'neath the midnight sun.

Palmer is a unique city. There are not many places that can claim some of the things that Palmer can. This poem has a couple of my favorite things that I could not figure out how to write a whole poem for them.

My favorite fact from Palmer is the Bingle. The government created a whole new currency because small businesses were the ones earning money and the government losing money. If the government paid the farmers with a coinage the businesses did not accept then the government would start making its money back. It did not work out the way they planned.

Fred Machentaz
A touch of pink, a splash of green,
Built on a canvas of ultramarine,
Coated in oil, makes a scene,
Of a white monarch, of the Arctic King,

For years the Painter's hand was thin,
Occasional portraits with colors blend,
But then Atwood brought life thickened,
So thickened the hand that the brush did
spin,

Passion flowed through every blood vein,
For Palmer, a town which some say he
made,
He fed other artists fame,
But in 02 his paint turned deathly gray,

Where has the painter and paint gone?
To show the vibrant orange of midnight
sun,
Was Machentaz the only one?
Nay "let's get em!" he cries to painters
young.

Fred Machentaz was a famous artist who lived near Trunk Road, on the west side of Palmer. He was a huge fan of the Palmer Moose football team, a supporter of local artists, and donated some of his land for the UA Mat-Su campus.

Fred, originally, did not seem to think his art was worth that much, but eventually a man named George Atwood changed that. The founder of the Anchorage Daily News organized a showcase of Fred Machentaz's art, where one piece was sold for 500 dollars, a lot of money back then. That was the push Machentaz needed to realize his worth, and get going.

Machentaz holds the valued position of being the first great local artist and is one to whom many of the locals should aspire to. There are other artists of varying calibers, but Machentaz will forever hold the title and the respect that goes with it.

3000-21™
Say Hi to these four robotic guys,
Life Is A Bore if you say Goodbye,
but if you watch for several Bright Signs,
you'll join Friends And A Campfire at night,

know these four can never be Replaced,
like rare Ice Crystals In Hyperspace,
though they say, "Let's Play Video Games",
which People often will say nowadays,

enter Astro Atoms Walkin' here,
Kid Amnezia forgets Forever,
for Nisumi Love Is On The Air,
42? Scatterbrained Man right there,

they're zooming Across The Metaverse,
with the smell of burnt astral Tires,
because they're Lost In The Metaverse,
escape 's The Last Place You Looked, well
darn,

they're taking The Path Of The Ninja,
a path we took When We Were Young kids,
they will Miss You as they speed off with,
Accelerated Motion engines.

This poem is published with permission from the band 3000-21™. When I was reading some of my poems at 203 Kombucha's open mic night one of the band members asked me if I took commissions. I of course said yes, I had developed a bit of a friendship with them by that point. It did present to me a sort of strange challenge though; how does one accurately represent a band in poetic form? I went through upwards of ten variations before I settled on the format you have read.

3000-21™ is a Palmer band that has a retro-futurist flavor to their music, due to the robot mascots for their band being time travelers. According to one of the musicians the four robots, Astro Atoms, Kid Amnezia, Nisumi, and 42, came from the future, went back to before the present, and recorded the music you can listen to today, or at least that is his head-canon.

George W. Palmer

"Το τέταρτο μπολ δεν είναι πια δικό μας[1]"
(Eubulus, Athenaeus Deipnosophistae)

When Valley farms were considered to be,
He advocated for wife's family,
That the planted foods colonists had
brought,
Would supplement the fish which wife had
caught,

He had married a Dena'ina woman,
A single mother with her own children,
And he traded fairly with her tribesmen,
And asked them to help tend to his garden,

------

[1] The fourth bowl is ours no longer (translated by a
friend).

Depending on what the garden produced,
Could affect what seeds the colonists used,
And with that and business he was inclined,
To be a sly worker through Christmas time,

But with disaster his life burned on fuel,
Consoled by his newly homemade White
Mule,
It caused him to kick and bellow at all,
This man's life was destroyed by alcohol,

He drank his first cup and he carried on,
He drank the second, but his love was gone,
After his third he refused to go sleep,
We know what happens after, and we
weep.

George W. Palmer is the man which the city of Palmer takes its name from. He was a businessman who had various establishments throughout the whole Southcentral region of Alaska. The first place he established was a trading post that was near where the George W. Palmer Bridge is now.

Perhaps in honor of his wife, or simply a sense of good morals, he always traded fairly with the local native population, and seemed to act as an advocate for them on occasion. One of the big things he did was influence what seeds they decided to ship for Palmer, so that the Dena'ina would benefit from the colony.

Since Palmer's life took a nosedive after he took to drink, I wanted to reference something that delt with restraint while drinking. Sadly I could not find any Native Alaskan stories that fit, so I had to humble myself and turn to the Greeks for my way.

The Matanuska Bard

A giant in form while meek in verse,
A farmer's palm worked with words,
He set to work at the till,
Where he worked till, he grew ill,
But his words survived him still,
Through a book which I have filled,
My mind with for a short time,
It beckons me to write rhymes,

He's the first poet to stand,
Upon Palmer's fertile land,
And gain a name to command,
Memories of those at hand,
All poets hereafter found,
On the Valley's frozen ground,
Owes high honor to Bob Klem,
First great poet on society's hem.

Bob Klem was a replacement colonist for the Matanuska Colony, but what is more important to me is that he was a poet, one of the first to get published in the Valley. His poems earned him some notoriety amongst the locals, who gave him the title "Matanuska Bard." One individual I talked with expressed a desire to have a statue cast of him at some point, a sentiment I now share.

The main thing going through my mind as I was writing this poem was how Bob Klem was the first. Just as every playwright must recognize Shakespeare, everyone of Palmer's poets must recognize Bob Klem. Of course, he is not known well enough for people to give him the honor that he deserves. Perhaps this book may help bring his name back to light.

www.ingramcontent.com/pod-product-compliance
Lightning Source LLC
Chambersburg PA
CBHW050758160726
48004CB00002B/619